HOW TO THRIVE POST

COVID-19

(Valuable insights for Business and Life Success during and after the

pandemic)

BY

Olumide Holloway

(King Olulu)

HOW TO THRIVE POST COVID-19

Copyright @2020 (Olumide Holloway)

Published in Nigeria by

Olumide Holloway

+2348025070892, +2348038315055, olulu4ever@gmail.com

www.wordup411ng.com

www.poetreel.com

olulu4ever@gmail.com

OTHER BOOKS BY OLUMIDE HOLLOWAY

1. The Untold Story of Uriah the Hittite.

2. Smoking Guns and Bleeding Streets.

3. The Way of the Lion.

4. Strategic Business Lessons from the Animal Kingdom.

5. The Poetpreneur.

6. Love Letters from a Poetpreneur.

7. Darkness can be very dark.

8. How many NO, make a YES?

All the books are available on Amazon.

The books are also on www.wordup411ng.com, and do subscribe to the website to receive notifications of news and updates by email.

Table of content

Acknowledgement

To the Great One that created wisdom, inspired King Solomon, and opened my eyes to Proverbs 1 to 15.

Dedication

To all wisdom seekers, may we find it and utilize it for the good of the world.

ABSTRACT

In this game, there are no happy endings. Play for as long as you can, and as you like it but time still outlasts you. Each wins usually pale in significance when you look across to see a playmate out of air.

In this game, there are no happy endings. So when they say smokers are liable to die young, the list of non-smokers is usually longer.

In this game, there are no happy endings. He said, give unto Caesar what is Caesar's. If Caesar must get his, do we expect the earth not to get back its own?

In this game, there are no happy endings. Eat right, drink right, pray right, do right, say right, give right, act right, be right,....still, memories are all that is left.

In this game, there are no happy endings. Time was created for us so only He that created time outlast time. Live or exist, when your time is up, you give it all up.

In this game, there are no happy endings. Enjoy and cherish the moments, that's all that matters at the end.

ABOUT THE AUTHOR

Olumide Holloway, better known as "Olulu, the King not from Zulu." is a 'POET-preneur', a Writer, Poet, and a Spoken Word Artist.

He loves reading, writing, dancing, making people happy, and generally having fun. He's passionate about Spoken Word Poetry, and his core purpose in life is to continually build capacity in people using Spoken Word Poetry as a tool and as a medium.

He is the promoter of WORD UP (a foremost Spoken Word Poetry event in Nigeria), and War Of Words (Nigeria's biggest slam poetry competition).

His purpose while here on Earth is building capacity in people using words and poetry.

He believes that everyone should do what they love, and love what they do. That way we can all be loving life, living in love, and getting paid for building businesses around our passion.

You can connect with him via:

Twitter @olulu4ever, Instagram @olulutheking, olulu4ever@gmail.com, +2348025070892

CHAPTER ONE

"It's easy money, a truckload of top-quality loot," he said and winked at me.

The other guys nodded in agreement. They had been drinking long before I got to the bar. I was still on my first bottle.

"What do we have to do?" I asked.

"We will do the hard part of ambushing them on their way from the bank. You go just be the driver."

"Will there be guns?" I asked.

"Yes na, we go raise hell, so that nobody go try form Super Man or avengers when we dey operate," he said aloud, and the others laughed.

He added, "join us for the time of your life. Cos with us, it's all brotherly love, equal sharing no cheating."

"Make I go piss, I dey come," I replied.

I stepped out of the compound the bar was in and entered the makeshift urinal erected on an open gutter.

"The more you get, the less you are."

I turned sharply to see who said that.

It was a lady with the gait of a headmistress. She looked back and I took a sharp breath.She was beautiful enough to be stunning, yet with a mature look that commands respect.

I felt wetness on my leg, so I turned back to finish what I was doing and I zipped up.

She stopped in front of the bar and spoke out loud:

"Young minds, how long will you wallow in ignorance? How long will you feed your cynicism? How long will you refuse to learn? I'm ready to invest in you, to teach and train you. I'm ready to tell you all I know. But una dey form "too woke", say you no see me or say una no understand my yarns. I hope say you no go laugh or yab this my advice, cos the day you go need am and call for me, I no go answer you, and no matter how hard you look, you no go see me. You hate knowledge and have nothing to do with the fear of God. You waste your time on schemes that promise easy money, and your minds fill up with cobwebs of foolishness. Don't you see what will happen? Carelessness kills, complacency is murder, and if you say you are killing time, you are committing suicide. Anyway sha, I don talk my own, whoever listens to me, will live safely and will be secure, without fear of evil."

She stopped, looked at me briefly, and then walked away in the opposite direction.

I stared at her retreating form. This was my first time seeing her, but I have heard about her before this day. The people in the hood call her "Lady Wisdom."

As I turned to walk away from the bar, I heard someone call my name.

CHAPTER TWO

She: Quitting your job was a bad decision; this crisis of COVID-19 has now made it worse. We are heading for rock bottom.

He: Rock bottom? Is that not a good place to start?

She: How is that one a good place to start?

He: At rock bottom, we can sink no further and that forms a good foundation to build on.

She: You don turn philosopher, abi? I am tempted to say my husband has gone mad o!!!

He: Oya come, let's reason together, what are the facts? What are the options?

She: Fact is that we are broke, so broke we can't even compare ourselves to church rats. Cos with churches now on lockdown, the rats have "ported" to greener pastures.

He: What are the options?

She: I no know o, you tell me.

He: R.T.I.A.C.L.S.S

She: What is this one now? Your kolo don dey mature o!
He: Receive, treasure, incline, apply, cry out, lift, seek, and search for.

She: I am still waiting for the sense in all this your nonsense.

He: Let me put it this way, what do we want? Why do we want it? How bad do we want it?

She: We want money na, abi what else?

He: What brings money? What is the principal thing?

She: Yes, I know wisdom is the principal thing, but do you know the address of the University of Wisdom or where is the College of Education for Wisdom located?

He: R.T.I.A.C.L.S.S

She: If you don't start making sense I will tell my father to return the dowry to you.

He: If we know wisdom is the principal thing and we truly desire it, then we simply seek out the wise ones physically and through their books. After all, he who walks with the wise will be wise, and a wise King once said that if we:—

1. Receive his words
2. Treasure his commands
3. Incline our ears to wisdom
4. Apply our heart to understanding
5. Cry out for discernment6. Lift our voice for understanding
7. Seek her (wisdom) as silver
8. Search for her as for hidden treasures

Then Lady Wisdom will be our close friend, brother knowledge will be our pleasant companion, good sense will scout ahead for danger, and insight will keep an eye out for us.

She: Hmmm.

He: The fact is we are at rock bottom, but as I said earlier the rock bottom is a good place to start. And since we have options, let's exercise them.

She: Hmmm

He: Can you trust me enough for us to try these options together?

She: Well, my father would have spent the dowry by now, so I am stuck with you. Besides, I need to stick around and ensure this "Lady Wisdom" is not a lady that her parent named Wisdom.

He: Nah, this wisdom is no physical woman.

She: I believe you, but I am also here to ensure it stays that way.

CHAPTER THREE

"Babe, I'm hungry o."

"Hungry ke? You just ate less than an hour ago. At this rate, you will need new trousers cos of your expanding waistline."

"I am sha hungry, and after the meal, me and you have unfinished business in ze oza room," I said winking at her.

"Haaa, no be me and you o. You better go and jog like other people are doing," she replied and ran into the kitchen as I tried to grab her.

My phone rang as I got up to go after her.

I picked it up and said, "hey Alex, how you dey?"

"Boss, I dey bam o. How are you are doing sir?"

"I am good, can only get better," I replied.

"Abeg boss quick one, I have read some of what you have written but I still dey burst my brain on how to successfully emerge from this ongoing crisis. Any pointers for your boy?"

"Hmmm..well, there is this Simon Sinek's video I watched recently and he said, "What value are you offering to people who buy your product and service, how will you do that in this new changing day and age? The opportunity is what would we become and not how to preserve what we had."

"OK. I dey with you baba," Alex responded.

I continued, "in this time and season, there is disruption everywhere and by the time COVID-19 is over, things won't revert to (the old) normal, there will be a new normal. The present-day jobs as we know it won't exist anymore, so new jobs will have to be created. Also, consumer habits and behaviours would have changed."

"How Sir?" He asked.

"Well, it is said that it takes 14 to 21 days to form a new habit and about 90 days to make it permanent. Most countries are on a minimum of 14 days lock-down, some lock-downs are more than 14 days and for those on an initial 14 days, extensions are very likely. Thus, new habits and behaviours are being formed during this lock-down period. Most pre-COVID 19 marketing strategies might not work post-COVID 19.

"So what are the practical things I can do in this present time and season?"

"Well, some things don't change, and the things that don't change are more or less principles. Let me share some with you:

- Don't lose your grip on love and truth; carve their initials on your heart.

- Don't withhold good from those to whom it is due. Never walk away from someone who deserves help. What goes around, comes around.

- Don't envy the oppressor and choose none of his/ her ways (i.e. don't adopt inhumane methods).

- Get wisdom and gain understanding through books, videos, audio materials, etc. Depth is key, so ensure you pay special focus to your craft and not on ongoing trends. 5. Trust in the Lord with all your heart, and lean not on your understanding. Don't assume you know it all.

He kept quiet for a moment and then he said, "Boss, wait small, let me get you right; I should gain understanding, but lean not on my understanding? Is that not an irony?"

I smiled as I replied, "well, good wisdom divorced from God can become a snare. Besides, if your wisdom and understanding were enough, you won't have any problem to contend with, would you? You probably would have created a vaccine or cure for COVID-19, right? Not leaning on your understanding means revelation is required from time to time. And revelation comes from God."

He queried further, "so my brain no go need to think again be that?"

"No o, you won't suspend your thinking when you get the revelation; you still need to think it through to see it through. These are times some humans who study innovation and change lives for. And just to be clear, innovation is trial and error. It is a clever way of solving a problem that involves experimenting. And when it comes to change, it is your preparation for it and your response to it that matters most."

"Ok, so if I get you right, I should get ready for change and be willing to innovate once the idea or revelation show face."

"Exactly, be ready and willing to re-invent yourself, so you can seize the opportunities that will surely arise from this crisis."

"Ok boss, I think my brain don receive air. Let me go and meditate small, and I will get back to you if I have more questions."

"You go pay for this consultation o."

"You na boss na, you no need my money."

"If I hear...!!!"

"No issues sir, I go do the do."

"Ok, go and sin no more."

He laughed, "thank you, sir. My regards to madam and the children."

CHAPTER FOUR

"Hello. Good day."

I looked at the WhatsApp message from the unknown number. I checked the picture, I did not recognize the face. I'm a member of some WhatsApp groups, so I checked if we had a group in common and none showed. "Well, no harm in replying," I said to myself.

"Hallos," I typed in response to the message.

"Hi. I'm Eratus from the Positive Mind Group"

"Oh ok. I'm Olulu. Nice to meet you Eratus."

"I'm an Accountant by profession but also a Rapper and Lyricist."

"Lol. I studied accounting, also have ACA. Left banking last year after more than 12 years for full-time writing and poetry."

"Wow! Interesting. I recently developed an interest in writing poems and articles."

"Hmmm."

"I will like to associate and learn from your experience and possibly see how I can earn from these skills of mine."

"No issues. I can do one of two things: Refer sites or books for you to go read, and you can work it out on your own. Or, alongside the above, I will give you assignments to do and follow up with you on it. However, number one is free, number two is affordable."

"That's quite a fair offer. Number 2 sure gonna come after I must have observed number 1. So I think we should start with one to introduce 2 later."

"Ok, no issues."

"And I was also wondering when episode 4 will be released."

"Episode 4?"

"Yes, the series you are doing on Proverbs."

"Well, I can give it to you right now. Besides, it will surely help you in writing poems and articles."

"Wow, I am all eyes."

"It's a short one. We can call it the Heart and the 3G."

"3G? Not 5G that everybody is talking about."

"Nah, this is one is 3G, and like one of my favourite speakers will say, the heart of the matter is a matter of the heart. Whatever you expose yourself to consistently will eventually enter your heart. And how do you expose yourself? It is by sight and sound, which is what you listen to and what you watch consistently, will end up dictating your mode of thinking and your way of life."

"As a man thinks in his heart..., abi?"

"Exactly. So if you want to upgrade your skills, you need to consciously and consistently expose yourself to materials and information that stir your imagination and arouse your creativity. The more knowledge you accumulate, the more likely the depth and beauty of your poems and articles. The keywords are consciously and consistently."

"Ok. But how does the 3G fit in?"

"Guide, Guard, Gauge."

"Hmmm."

"If you guide your heart, it will guard your life and will serve as a gauge i.e. evaluate where you are, from time to time. So let your heart retain wise words, keep wisdom in your heart, and keep your heart with all diligence. In other words: take wisdom to heart, learn knowledge by heart, and keep a vigilant watch over your heart."

"How do you see these things?"

"You see what you diligently look for."

"True. So what books and sites do you recommend for me?"

"I will send book titles and sites later today when I get to my laptop."

"Ok, cool. Thanks for your time."

"Thank you too."

"I will buzz you later for the info you promised."

"No issues, I am at your service."

"Lol. Thanks again."

"Ok bro, stay alert, stay safe."

"You too sir."

CHAPTER FIVE

"Ore, I've been following your recent posts and the thing dey make sense. But can you do one (using your source document i.e. Proverbs) along the line of skills that will be relevant during the full emergence of A.I and/ or post COVID 19."

Me response:

A simple Google search states that future work skills include:

1. Complex problem-solving.

2. Critical thinking.

3. Creativity.

4. Cognitive flexibility.

5. Social skills.

So let's take complex problem solving as our case study.

But first, let me stay by stating two assumptions:

- Experiences differ, but principles are universal. However, to every rule, there is an exception.

- People sometimes categorise problems into two: Common and Complex. But I believe a common problem will be complex as long as there is a dearth of knowledge to solve it. And a complex problem is as complex as the level of your ignorance.

Are we are clear on the assumptions?

Then let's proceed.

In problem-solving, there is a process flow.

We can call the process flow the 3Rs.

These are:

Reasons

Results

Remedy for the problem.

Let's take them one by one as follows:

What are the "Reasons" for the problem?

A. You hate instruction

B. Your heart despised correction

C. You did not listen to mentors

D. Or take your teachers seriously.

What are the "Results"?

Loss

Pain

Failure

Regrets

Waste

Injury

Death (worst case scenario)

What is the "Remedy" to the problem?

Pay close attention to Wisdom (he who walks with the wise will be wise. The wise can be found physically or via their products).

Listen closely to insights (Basically, learn from other people's experience. First does not always mean best).

Acquire a taste for good sense (in other words, bless/ freshen up the flowing fountain of your "mind").

In situations, where it a skill related/specialized problem, we can further break it down as follows:

Rejoice with the wife of your youth...let her breasts satisfy you at all times (in another context, don't ever quit taking delight in her body).

Never take her love for granted.

Let's rewrite the above:

Take delight in the skills you acquired in your youth.

Never quit being passionate about it, so dig deeper and acquire depth by following up with innovation in that sector/ industry.

Never take the knowledge you have for granted, because so many people don't have it, yet they need it. You can sell the knowledge

I hope the above makes sense to you and will be of help also.

Cheers.

CHAPTER SIX

"Guy, you no go fit bamboozle me today. I know what next you are going to write about."

"You do?"

"Yes o, you are going to write about the ANTS."

"True that."

"And since na John Maxwell Bible you dey use, I know you are going to write about Leadership Lessons from the ANTS."

"Lol, so you think I will simply copy and paste?"

"No. I know you stay fresh and original, but you fit use the Leadership Lessons as your base. Abi?"

"Nope. Not at all."

"Haa."

"See, when I read to write, I look for what was not written."

"O se, Sherlock Holmes lomo!!!"

"Lol. Do you know what jumped at me when I read about the Ants?"

"Yarn me."

"Business Models."

"Business Models ke? Not leadership lessons?"

"I try to read a lot to feed my mind with data. This allows my mind to cross-reference topics with the data in it, to find a pattern. I think the process is called Intuitive creativity."

"Ok."

"The pattern I saw was all about Business Models. Cos the key verse was, "go to the ant...consider her ways and be wise." This suggests that we should study, observe, research, and learn. The next verses after that is a summary i.e. an appetizer, and not the main course. "

"Oya wetin be Business Model? "

"It's the representation of different ways of adding value to goods and/or services to earn income. It is the multiple possibilities to add value and generate revenue."

"And what is the Ants' Business Model?"

"For most ants, the survival of their Queen(s) is their sole purpose, and the Queen's function in life is to lay thousands of eggs that will ensure the survival of the colony. In our case, the Queen represents the cash flow of a business. Without cash flow, there is no business."

"You are doing well, carry on."

"And when we come to the eating habits, Ants are predators, scavengers and herbivores. These eating habits are regarded as the Business Models that Ants adopt to survive and thrive. The eating habits utilized by the Ant are based on location, availability (of prey), and prevailing circumstance."

"Hmmm, correct."

"So given the ongoing crisis in the world, most of the existing business models are failing. Thus, like Ants, business models need to be changed or modified. So, first thing first, businesses need to go digital, have an online presence that enables them to work and service their customers and clients remotely. Businesses need to change their approach to conform to current realities."

"Can you give practical examples?"

"One, the market for fashion attires is low at this time, so tailors/ fashion designers can start designing, sewing, and selling fashionable nose masks. Two, for businesses who want people to download financial/ business mobile apps, they can do "value for value" giveaways online. Three, Schools and their teachers should upload educational videos online so that their pupils continue learning from home. Four, in addition to three, Schools and Churches should note that some people try to manage data, so the conversion of videos to downloadable audio will increase the reach to people who don't download videos or watch videos online. I only watch WhatsApp videos on my laptop with my WIFI and not on my phone. Five, for the knowledge-selling business, Podcasting is an option, and this can free or subscription-based."

"Hmm."

"Face to face selling won't work at this time, so learn to pivot. Change or modify your Business Model appropriately."

"This one na Learning Business Models from Ants."

"Lol, or something like that."

"I dey gbadun your writing ore, keep the fire burning."

"O se bro, na God be the Boss, I am just the Bus."

"Na so. "

"Stay Safe bro and Jah bless."

"You too ore, stay alert, stay alive. "

CHAPTER SEVEN

"No matter how hard you search, a man's destiny can never be found on Google."

This line had been on his mind for a week. He had heard it on YouTube while watching the performance of a poet called Habeeb Ajijola.

"Baba God o, pick up, pick up," he said silently, lifting his hands to the sky as he walked down to the bus-stop.

He had finished his afternoon shift at the bank where he was employed as a security guard. He had joined the bank six months earlier after two years of been jobless. The pay was not much, but being six feet tall, dark and handsome made him a favourite of the female staff and customers of the bank, so he got plenty of tips. And being a ladies man, he knew how to turn on the charm with his smile and well-spoken English.

He stood at the bus stop alone for over 5 minutes before remembering Okada and Keke Napep had been banned over the weekend. He shook his head as he thought about the distance he had to cover to get a bus that will take him to his area.

Just as he was about to start walking when he noticed a white Lexus SUV with tinted glasses reversing to the spot he was at. The car stopped beside him and the window came down. He stooped to look inside the vehicle.

His eyes first caught sight of her exposed thighs, then her cleavage (as exposed by a low-cut blouse) before he saw the face of a beautiful light skin woman smiling at him. He liked what he saw, so he smiled back.

"Good afternoon ma," he said.

"Good afternoon dear, how are you," she replied.

"I am doing well ma."

"Where are you headed? Maybe I can drop you off."

"I want to get a bus to Lekki gate and then another to Ketu."

"I am going to Gbagada, would Iyana Oworo be okay for you?"

"It's perfect ma."

"Ok, come in."

He opened the door and sat down beside her.

"Hope you don't mind if I quickly branch home to pick up my bag and stuff before we head off," she said as she engaged the gear and drove on.

"No problem ma."

"You work at the bank?" she asked.

"Yes."

He glanced at her and their eyes met briefly before she turned back to the road.

"You are a handsome young man," she said.

"Thank you ma."

"Your girlfriend is a lucky girl," she said smiling.

He chuckled and replied, "I don't have a girlfriend."

"You don't? A fine boy like you! I don't believe that," she exclaimed.

"No romance without finance ma," he replied, and they both laughed.

She stopped the car in front of a huge gate, honked twice and the gate opened sideways.

"Hope you don't mind coming inside to have a drink or two, while I quickly shower and change."

He glanced at her left hand and saw the wedding ring.

"I don't want no trouble ma," he said.

"My husband is not home' he is away on business, and he won't be back for a month," she replied smiling sweetly.

He was quiet and did not move.

She threw her arms around him and kissed him, boldly took his arm, and said, "I've prepared a romantic dinner. For today I scanned around if I would see you, hoping to catch sight of your face—and here you are! I've spread fresh, clean sheets on my bed, colorful imported linens. My bed is aromatic with spices and exotic fragrances. Come, let's make love all night, and spend the night in blissful lovemaking!"

With her enticing speech, she caused him to yield, with her flattering lips she seduced him.

Immediately he went with her, like an Ox goes to the butcher shop, or like a male Goat lured into an ambush and then shot with an arrow. Like a bird runs into a trap, he did not know it would cost his life.

For she has cast down many wounded, and all who were slain by her were strong men. Her house is the way to hell, descending to the chambers of death.

CHAPTER EIGHT

"Outrageous nonsense!!!"

"Ogbeni Kunle, wetin do you? Where you thief this grammar?"

Kunle: Why you kill the guy na?

Me: Which guy? Abeg o, I no kill anybody o.

Kunle: I was just starting to enjoy the story, you come kill the guy.

Me: Who you dey talk about?

Kunle: The guy for your last story, you just make am die like that. Just because he follow fine woman.

Me: I dey follow the laid down storyline na, as written by King Solomon.

Kunle: But na so person dey die?

Me: Well, from lust to sin, and when sin is fully grown, it becomes from sin to death.

Kunle: Nawa o. Anyway, I dey reason how you go write the next chapter because I no see which story you go take talk am.

Me: You get any ideas for me?

Kunle: Correct man, I think so you no go ask.

Me: Oya, fire on.

Kunle: You can say, "One day I was seated in a crowded bar, enjoying my bottle of beer and someone whispered in my ears, I love those who love me, and those who look for me, find me."

Me: Hmm, go on.

Kunle: "So I looked up to see a lovely looking matured woman smile at me and walked past me. Normally, I would be staring at her behind, but my mind was trying to decode what she said earlier. Suddenly, I remembered that I have seen her before; people in this hood call her Lady Wisdom. So I got up and went after her."
You dey feel me?

Me: I dey feel you.

Kunle: "Na so I pursue the woman, sorry, I mean, so I went after her and caught up with her by the door. She turned and said aloud; Wealth and Glory accompany me, also substantial Honor and a Good Name. My benefits are worth more than a big salary, even a very big salary; the returns on me exceed any imaginable bonus. You can find me on Righteous Road—that's where I walk— at the intersection of Justice Avenue, handing out life to those who love me, filling their arms with life—armloads of life!"

Me: Bro, you don dey quote bible o.

Kunle: Wetin you wan quote before?

Me: Ok, oya continue.

Kunle: "Everyone turned to look at her, for her voice over-shadowed the noise in the bar. Everywhere went silent. Who are you, someone asked. And she replied, "God sovereignly made me—the first, the basic— before he did anything else. I was brought into being a long time ago, well before Earth got its start. I arrived on the scene before Ocean, yes, even before Springs and Rivers and Lakes. Before Mountains were sculpted and Hills took shape, I was already there, newborn; Long before God stretched out Earth's Horizons, and tended to the minute details of Soil and Weather, and set the Sky firmly in place, I was there."

Me: Hmmm.

Kunle: Wetin be hmm?

Me: Nothing, fire on.

Kunle: "She is drunk, someone said, and another shouted, all na wash jor. And a third voice said, abeg woman, comot make we see road, carry your super story go another place."

Me: Ok, go on.

Kunle: "She looks around, shakes her head and looks directly into my eyes and said, whoever finds me finds life, and obtains favor from the Lord. But if you wrong me, you damage your very soul. For all those who hate me are flirting with death. And she turned around and exited the bar."
Dazall.

Me: The end? Hmm. Not bad, you try small. I am impressed.

Kunle: Correct, I'm happy you like it. So you go use am?

Me: Not sure yet.

Kunle: Why na? Shebi the thing make sense and since you never get your own concept, you fit borrow this one.

Me: Well, sometimes you don't have to tell a story, just tell a story about wanting to tell a story.

CHAPTER NINE

"I'm tired of being broke," Bayo blurted out.

The 4 guys seated opposite him around the table looked at him. They had been deep in discussion largely ignoring him.

"So wetin you wan do?" One of the guys called AK asked.

"Dunno jare, still trying to figure it out," Bayo responded.

"Wetin you dey figure out, align with us and we go share you the loot," AK replied.

"I no fit dey rob and do 419 like you guys. I can't but pity the victims, their loss, their pain."

"Well, God puts down one and elevate another, since promotion comes from God," AK stated with a mischievous smile.

"Haa, no be this kain way God dey promote o."

"You be God? You don forget that He works in mysterious ways."

"Well, your way no pure. There must be another way." Bayo replied.

"Go meet that woman na, the one wey dey always shout say she sabi the way," AK said in a mocking tone.

"Na the first sensible thing you don talk be this."

"You better waka before I perforate your belly."

Bayo stood up and left them at the bar. He headed for the house of the lady AK had referred to. He was not sure what to expect, but he felt in his guts that he was doing the right thing.

15 minutes later, he got to the gate of a simple but well built fully detached duplex. The duplex had a design that made it look like it was supported by 7 hewn timbers.

Bayo noticed the gate to the compound was ajar, so he pushed it open and walked to the front door.

About 6 feet from the door, it opened. The Lady stared at him for a while, as if reading his mind.

"Good afternoon ma," he greeted.

"How are you doing?" She responded.

"I am fine."

"Are you hungry?" She asked.

"Em...em...not really ma."

"Come with me, come have dinner with me. I've prepared a wonderful spread of Party Jollof Rice, fried plantain, roasted Goat, and carefully selected wines."

"I did not come for food ma."

"I know the food you seek is not physical. You seek to leave your impoverished confusion, go in the way of understanding and live a life of meaning."

"How do you know what I seek?"

"You came here by yourself without invitation, didn't you?"

"Yes, I did."

"I don't waste my time on scoffers; else all I'll get for my pains is abuse. But if I correct those who care about life, that's different—they'll love me for it! So I save my breath for the wise, so they'll be wiser for it. I tell good people what I know and they profit from it. For the fear of the Lord is the beginning of wisdom and the knowledge of the Holy One is understanding."

"That means you can help me," Bayo chipped in.

"Yes. For it's through me, Lady Wisdom, that your life deepens and years of life added to you. If you are wise, you are wise for yourself, and wisdom will permeate your life; but if you mock life, life will mock you. So come with me, let's dine together and reason together, your set time is now."

CHAPTER TEN

"I counted body parts."

"Huh? You did what?"

"Well, when unsure of how to proceed, I start to count."

"Ok, so of all things to count, na body parts you see count?"

"I read the whole chapter 10; it was full of wise sayings by one of the wisest men to ever live. And I wondered, where do I start from? Which one of the wise sayings do I expatiate on?"

"I still dey wait for how body parts came to play."

"Well, after reading and re-reading KJV, NKJV, and the Message version, my experience as a Business Analysis and Strategist came into play. I settled for NKJV and found that the word "Hand" was used twice, "Head" was used twice, "Tongue" was used three times, "Lips" was used five times and then "Mouth" was used six times."

"So the hand, head, tongue, lips, and mouth are the body parts you counted?"

"Yes."

"Ok, so what do we make of what you have counted?"

"The correlation between the words most used i.e. tongue, lips, and mouth, is what you say, which is your "speech." This means, what we say and don't say, means a lot."

"Hmmm, ok."

"How do we further expand on this?"

"You tell me."

"I decided to borrow a concept by Leke Alder. In a recent interview, Leke Alder had stated that in coming up with strategies for companies and individuals, his firm makes use of SWOT analysis and FAD analysis. Most of us know what SWOT analysis is all about. However, FAD analysis is a concept developed by Leke Alder's firm, so it is unpopular."

"What is FAD analysis?"

"FAD means Fear, Accusation, and Doubt. This usually applied to companies by asking three questions, which are: one, what can cause Fear about the company in the market? Two, what can lead to accusations about the company in the market? And three, what are the things that create doubt in the minds of the customers/ market?"

"How do you apply this FAD analysis to King Solomon's wise sayings?"

"I thought long and hard about that and I decided to flip it. So I replaced Fear, Accusation, and Doubt, with Faith, Appreciation, and Dedication."

"Ok."

"If we are to apply the flipped FAD analysis to our speech, we will ask questions like one, does your speech invoke Faith? In other words, "the mouth of the righteous is a well of life, but violence covers the mouth of the wicked. Two, does your speech lead to Appreciation? In other words, "Wisdom is found on the lips of him who has understanding, but a rod is for the back of him who is devoid of understanding." And three, does your speech or lack of it, convey Dedication? In other words, "the mouth of the righteous brings forth wisdom, but the perverse tongue will be cut out."

"Correct, you strategically flip the script to make sense of it."

"Na so my guy, na so."

"I enjoyed it, thanks for sharing."

"Thank you too."

CHAPTER ELEVEN

"Bros, how we wan take survive this ongoing crisis? This lockdown is turning to a knockdown o."

"And you think I have the answers?"

"Shebi na you dey consult with King Solomon and remix Proverbs to take provide answers. Oya consult again and tell us how we go survive and thrive afterward."

"Lol. No one has all the answers. Most experts talking right now on post-COVID are doing "guesstimate.""

"So make we just siddon dey watch?"

"No matter how hard the exams you were to do in school, you still prepared for it, didn't you? Well, this is one of life's critical exam, get prepared."

"How na? COVID no be the exam?"

"It's part of it, but post-COVID is the main paper."

"But we never even know whether we go even survive the thing sef."

"No war takes everybody away. There will always be survivors."

"Ok, so how we go pass this kain exam?"

"Where there is no counsel, the people fall; but in the multitude of counselors, there is safety. So listen to people who can add value to what you already know. They don't have all the answers, but they can provide a certain level of direction."

"Ok, what else can I do?"

"Stay relevant and if possible, indispensable. For the generous soul will be made rich and he or she who waters will also be watered."

"Abeg, break this one down. How does one stay relevant in this time and this season?"

"Check up on people, engage in conversation, cos loneliness and depression can kill at this time. Offer support, financial if possible. Offer discounts, if you can afford it. Volunteer your time, gift, and skill whether physically or from home. Just ensure you add value as much as you can."

"Even from home?"

"Yes, your phone can serve as your work station. Just add value one way or the other, cos he who earnestly seeks good finds favour. But trouble will come to him that seeks evil."

"You don take style consult with King Solomon and remix Proverbs, as usual, abi?"

"Ore, in uncertain times like this, I look for things that stay constant and Principles rarely change no matter the situation. So all I try to do is to find the underlying principle and then I apply it."

"Principles rarely change? With the many many technology changes."

"Technology is the drama, the principle stays the same."

"Technology is the drama ke?"

"Yes, it is."

"Abeg, break it down."

"No worry, I will do that later. Let's keep it short today."

"Ok bros. Stay safe"

"You too, stay alert, stay alive."

CHAPTER TWELVE

"This decade will be governed by Revelation and not Education."

"The next level of power is always hidden in your prevailing level of power."

"Hope is not a strategy, it's a dependent variable that requires other factors to survive."

He had stayed up all night pondering on the above statements made by Olakunle Soriyan during an IG live interview.

"So we can't just wish this crisis away or hope things will just work out themselves," he thought and then exclaimed aloud, "Kai, faith must work hard to work out."

He picked his phone and called a friend.

"Hi Olulu, wetin dey sup," he said.

"Hey Enahoro, nothing much o, na lockdown things," his friend replied.

"Same here o, but wetin man fit do na? We can't just sit down and be hoping things will work out."

"Well, I've been listening to a lot of my mentors from afar and one question the lectures have raised in my mind is, what is the good for me in the midst of this situation?"

"And do you have an answer to this question?" Enahoro asked.

"In a way, yes."

"Please share."

"The lazy man does not roast what he took in hunting, but diligence is man's precious possession."

"This one na proverb o, abeg explain."

"Well, in it are 3 things - value creation, value addition, and value remuneration."

"Break it down some more."

"Hunting and getting the animal is value creation, skinning, cutting, and frying/ roasting the animal is value addition, and selling the processed animal is value remuneration."

"That one na Hunter, how does it work for other professions?"

"Writing is value creation, editing, proofreading, and publishing as a paperback and/or E-book is value addition, and selling it is value remuneration."

"Ok."

"While the part that says diligence is man's precious possession, is stating the need for consistency. Thus, you have to always engage in value creation, value addition, and value remuneration day in, day out."

"Even in this crisis period? How do I even know what to engage in? Or that I should continue doing what I do?"

"Well, a man will be commended according to his wisdom. So ask, and ye shall receive."

"Hmm, no wonder Mr. Soriyan said this decade will be governed by Revelation and not Education."

"Exactly."

"Ok na. Let me get to work on value creation. Thanks Olulu."

"I'm always at your service."

CHAPTER THIRTEEN

"Bro, what's the plan? Are you going to make it into a book?"

"Huh? Make what into a book?"

"This your yarns about Proverbs. Would it come out as a book?"

"Truth be told, I was just writing to test myself and decipher things unseen by the naked eyes. But a few people have requested to have it as a book."

"So you go do am as book?"

"If people pay in advance, yes ke."

"Hmm, sounds fair enough."

"Abi na, wetin man go do."

"And the things you wan decipher, you don get them?"

"Yes, I believe so. After all, there must be something to learn from one of the wisest men that ever lived."

"So wetin your eye see?"

"I saw the 3Ls."

"You don start this your coding again. Which one be L "meta" again?"

"Lol, the 3Ls are life, light, and love."

"What did you learn about them?"

"Well for starters, "the teaching of the wise is a fountain of life" and "sound thinking makes for gracious living." Wisdom allows us to push life into vision, projects, organizations, groups, etc by our presence, skills, and character. "

"Ok, fair enough. Is the "light" the same as the one from NEPA?"

"Lol, you wish. This light is insight. The kind of insight that one has to diligently seek for cos it is not found in common places. That's why it is said, "he who walks with wise men, will be wise." For the wise ones help shed light on issues and decisions that need to be made."

"I know say the love part na love your neighbor as thyself, no be so?"

"Love is all-encompassing, so it can also be "a refusal to correct is a refusal to love; love your children by disciplining them."

"Hmmm, L meta! Life, light, and love."

"Yesso."

"But how do you see all these things in this Proverbs wey we don read tire."

"If I tell you, I would have to kill you."

"Kill me ke?"

"Na joke na. It's a way of saying I no go tell you."

"Ok o, Sha keep it coming, I dey gbadun you."

"Oya pay for the book na."

"Send me your account number."

"Correct man, this is sweet music to my ears."

"You like money o."

"Who no like better thing? After all, money answers all things."

"But no be everything dey ask question o!"

CHAPTER FOURTEEN

"Hello, ma."

"Hello dear."

"Mami, good morning ma."

"Good morning Omo mi, bawo ni."

"Fine ma."

"How is everybody? Your husband and children?"

"We are all fine ma, we bless the Lord."

"Hallelujah to God."

"Yes o. This one that you are calling this early, hope no issues ma."

"Not really dear, I just felt I should have a heart to heart discussion with you."

"What is it ma?"

"Well, I'm sure you know the man is the head of the house and the chief provider for the family."

"Yes, ma."

"As his help-mate and in this present-day realities, a woman should also be making her own money o."

"But you know I have a job ma."

"Yes, I know. But you also should have a small business by the side. So that you are not dependent on only one source. What if your husband's business has issues or God forbid, what if his health is affected?"

"But mami, where is the time and energy for a side hustle?"

"My dear, a wise woman builds her house, but the foolish pulls it down with her hands."

"Mama, are you yabbing me ni?"

"No o, why would I? But I see your forwarded messages on what is up, as well as, your comments and posts on Facebook."

"Yes, but I only do it to keep in touch with family and friends."

"Well, hard work pays off; mere talk puts no bread on the table. And the crown of the wise is their riches, but the foolishness of fools is folly."

"Haa mami, this one you are using parables or is it Proverb to yab me is not fair o."

"I no yab you dear. But the truth is not a cough syrup."

"Ok ma, I will give it a shot."

"That's my girl, my God will help you."

"Amen."

"Wisdom rests in the heart of him/ her who has understanding, and I pray God will grant you deeper insights from this discussion."

"Amen. Thank you ma."

"Thank you omo mi. I will be calling for a progress report o."

"Kai, mami you still dey do like a principal."

"Well, once a principal always a principal. This one is homework, so I will expect a progress report."

"No problem ma. I will surely work on it."

"Ok dear, my love to the children and greet your husband for me."

"I will ma, take care of yourself ma and my love to Daddy."

"I will tell him. Bye-bye."

"Bye, ma."

CHAPTER FIFTEEN

"I miss you," she said.

"I miss you more," he replied.

"I love you," she said.

"I love you more," he responded.

She smiled and held the phone closer to her ears.

"I can't wait to be married to you, Mr. Macaulay."

"Me lady, right here beside me is where you should be, if not for this lockdown."

"If only my folks had allowed us to do the traditional wedding early this year, I would be in your arms right now."

"Aww, God knows best dear, God knows best," he said softly.

"So what were you doing before I called?" She asked.

"I was reading a book titled Storytelling the Book of Proverbs by King Olulu," he replied.

"Hmm, sounds interesting. What's it about?"

"Well, this chapter says communication equals conflict or communication equals collaboration. This applies to business, marriage, and life itself."

"So any specific things to do to aid our communication?"

"For starters, a soft answer turns away wrath, but a harsh word stirs up anger."

"You know I talk so soft my love."

"Me lady, it is not what you say, it is how you say it."

They both laughed.

"So what else did you gain from the book?"

"Kind words heal and help; cutting words wound and maim."

"Ok."

"Perception is key too," he said.

"Perception?"

"Yes, cos perspective words spread knowledge; fools are hollow - there's nothing for them. To that add this one, the empty-headed treat life as a plaything; the perspective grasps life's meaning and make a go of it."

"Communication, perception, and what else my love?" She asked.

"Listen to good sound advice. For without counsel, plans go awry. But in the multitude of counselors, they are established. Also, the ear that hears the rebukes of life will abide among the wise."

"Hmmm."

He continued, "my best part is, the fear of the Lord is the instruction of wisdom, and before honor is humility."

"Before honor is humility," she echoed.

"Yesso, na so."

"This King Olulu must be a wise man," she said.

"Well, he said he does not claim to be a wise man but he loves to walk with wise ones," he replied.

"Hmm, I like him."

"Like him ke? You are liking another man and telling me."

"Mr. Macaulay, you know and I know you know that you are the only man for me, and I love you."

"I love you more."

"I miss you."

"I miss you more."

BONUS SCRIPT

My teeth bit my tongue as I was chewing on the sandwich. I was hungry so I continued to munch away.

The fact that I needed the food to overcome the hunger made the bite on my tongue forgivable.

I called my wife.

"Darling, I'm sorry about this morning. Please forgive me, I should not have shouted at you and used such harsh words, I'm sorry. Let's go out tonight, Chinese restaurant, then we go see a movie and tomorrow I'll take you shopping."

She said, "wow, I'll love you."

Me: What's wrong with your voice? Do you have a cold?

She: No, I don't have a cold and I also don't have a husband.

Me: Bolanle is that you?

She: No, my name is Nkechi.

Me: Isn't that 08038315055?

She: This is 08038315855

Me: Oh, I'm sorry, I called the wrong number.

She: No problem, it happens.

Me: Why did you not say something earlier?

She: Well, I was enjoying hearing a loving husband.

THE END

REFERENCES

1. Proverbs 1 to 15
2. Holy Bible – King James Version
3. The Maxwell Leadership Bible – New King James Version
4. The Message Bible

THE UNTOLD STORY OF URIAH THE HITTITE.

CHAPTER ONE

"Hey bro, welcome back," Gareb said as he entered the tent. "I heard them hailing you earlier but I was depositing manure into the soil. How you dey?"

They shook hands and hugged.

"I dey alright my brother, all correct, no shaking," replied Uriah.

He sat down on his bed facing Gareb, who leaned on the table.

"How was the City and home front?" Gareb asked.

"Fine."

"So what did the King want to see you for?"

"To be honest, I really don't know. We did not talk about anything serious or discreet. We did more drinking than talking. I guess he misses the Warfront," Uriah replied.

They both laughed.

"But at least you got to gum body and had a nice time with madam, " Gareb said as he smiled and winked.

"Nah, I did not go home. I slept at the door of the King's house with all the servants of my King."

"Kilode? Why? You for go enjoy wifey's company"

"My guy, the King suggested that too. But I told him that the ark and Israel and Judah are dwelling in tents, and my Lord Joab and the servants of my King are encamped in the open field. Shall I then go to my house to eat and drink, and to lie with my wife? As the King's soul lives, I will not do that," said Uriah.

"Wow," exclaimed Gareb as he looked at Uriah in astonishment.

Uriah added, "I just did not feel right about it. I had a bad feeling about the whole visitation and insistence that I go home. I would rather be here at the battlefront with you guys then be at home frolicking with wifey."

They both laughed.

Just then, Zaharai, the armor-bearer of Joab, entered into the tent. "Uriah, my Lord Joab will see you now."

Together they marched to the tent of Joab.

"Good day sir," Uriah said as he entered the tent.

"Welcome back Soldier," Joab replied and added, "how was the home front?"

"All correct Sir."

"I am sure you enjoyed Madam's cooking and the after-hours things," Joab said with a smile.

Uriah smiled but said nothing.

"Any news from my King David?" Joab asked.

"Yes sir, he said to give you a letter," Uriah replied. He removed a sealed letter from the waist pouch and placed it in Joab's outstretched hand.

Joab checked to be sure the seal was unbroken. He then opened the letter, read it, and frowned. He looked up to see Uriah watching him and their eyes locked for a few seconds. Out of respect, Uriah blinked and looked away.

"Anything the matter sir?" Uriah asked.

Joab turned his back on him and said, "Go back to your tent soldier; I will call you if I need you."

Uriah hesitated for a moment. He was sure Joab's voice sounded like a man in pain and in tears. "Ok sir," he said and left the tent.

Joab held the letter in both hands and raised it above his head. "Why my King? Why?" He muttered as tears flowed down his cheeks.

Joab cried all night and found no sleep or rest to console his troubled soul.

CHAPTER TWO

(About 30 years earlier)

"Hey Uriah, no farm today?"

He looked to his right and saw Inarahsu and Daraksu walking towards him. They were twin brothers and the sons of one of the richest merchants in their village.

"No, no farm today," he replied, looking at Inarahsu as the twins stopped in front of him.

"Why? Don't you want to be a farmer like your father?" Asked Daraksu.

"I don't want to be a farmer."

"But your father is a farmer, you will probably end up a farmer," insisted Inarahsu.

"No," responded Uriah sternly.

The boys looked at him strangely.

"Why don't you want to be a farmer?"

"I've not seen myself as a farmer in my dreams."

One of the boys laughed and said, "so you think you are now like Joseph the dreamer because your papa give you Hebrew name. No deceive yourself, you be Hittite, not a Hebrew."

Daraksu added, "I can't wait to see your papa's face when you tell him you don't want to be a farmer."

Uriah looked at them and said slowly, "someday you will hear and see my greatness."

The 2 boys looked at each other and then laughed so hard, they fell over rolling on the floor.

Uriah walked away from them, he knew he wanted more than this life of being a farmer. He just was not sure what else he would do.

Uriah was the 3rd boy out of 5 children. He had two elder brothers and two younger sisters. It was less than two years between the ages of each of the children.

His father had a farm and his two brothers were already working with his father, as well as, developing their own farm. It was expected that Uriah would also start on his own farm once he reached the age of 18. For now, he was mainly in charge of the two Cows that lived in their home.

'You are back early," his mother remarked as he stormed into the common room.

"I don't want to be a farmer," he replied with teeth clenched.

She turned and looked at him. She then moved close to him and hugged him. At five feet 9 inches, he was the shortest male in the family but he was still taller than his mother.

She held him close and said softly, "when the voice of greatness calls you, be unafraid to answer." She drew back, smiled, and said aloud, "now go milk the Cows else you no go chop tonight."

He smiled back and went to milk the cows.

OTHER BOOKS BY OLUMIDE HOLLOWAY

1. The Untold Story of Uriah the Hittite.

2. Smoking Guns and Bleeding Streets.

3. The Way of the Lion.

4. Strategic Business Lessons from the Animal Kingdom.

5. The Poetpreneur.

6. Love Letters from a Poetpreneur.

7. Darkness can be very dark.

8. How many NO, make a YES?

All the books are available on Amazon.

The books are also on www.wordup411ng.com, and do subscribe to the website to receive notifications of news and updates by email.